DRUGS FOR A TORTURED MIND

I wandered the streets...a whore for love
...my poems, a pastime for the ladies
and wrote my lonely heart at night.

The dogs, the cats, the rats with rabies
encircled me and drank my love
and ate my money with a knife

and buried bones and words I shared
and sent me to another life
...a pigeon in the morning light
of New York 's central square.

COMPUTER POETRY TILL MORNING

Fatigue come the night, come deep
...a burning fatigue to tired to sleep!
Instead of this thoughts wander off,
kick the sheets and start to cough
smoke and weep and pace the floor
sense the creaking of the door
and chase those flickerings of light
within that deep fatigue of night.

ABSTRACTS OF PURGATORY

In a dozen or so paintings
in this case made of muted colors
...light and shade and anguish.
Or the block print white on black
whose inversions mirror something dark
pulled from the soul...its bloodied sack

...the pigeon flies
...the raven and the lark
go mooning afternoon and evening
with their repetitious song

...for you have done the sorrow of my face
along with all the spirit and the meaning
of a tired race
of broken men

as if returning from the factory mill
into a final house in the country
to a place in a vacant glen.

A ROOM UPSTAIRS BLOOMS DARK

A room upstairs blooms dark
and the mirror hung along with art
gives a quietness and suffusion
to the music in my heart.

Fifty years of cigarettes
...the slow breath
in the Autumn air
timed in wheezes
which reflect in ways like death
flickering computer radio and soft guitar
inside from Autumn breezes.

Soft!...the darkness gathers
...and strangely seems to help me
...seems to help like bonfire chant
...seems to help like clouds covering a star
...seems like some defeat
more real and beautiful than victory
in all its tragic error.

The fire in me will smoke
and the days will cough and joke
and in such darkness tears
are somehow gone
and somehow hidden
from this strange rooms magic mirror.

A BUM GOES HOME FOR THE HOLIDAYS

Frosty is the nitwit mind
which stumbles Autumn
leaves... and beer
bristling at the lips
the savage poet coughs and spits
the chill within his wayward song
the song within his likewise leer
on such a wondrous holiday
...turkey day or Halloween
soaked in rum
and drenched in wine

..."I paint a hollow Saturday with words."
so moans the poet blind
stumbling on the freezing wind
...stumbling ever southward
after birds.

AN ART LIKE THE SPANISH ISLANDS

Your sweet and ancient nudity
while the computer plays a serenade
of classical guitar

...love is firm like a tree
and daylight is a star
brightening a planet full of blue.

With the fire in our eyes
and your paintings on the wall

as long as I live
I will dream of you.

HOW NOT TO BE A LOSER

Run with the dogs
fart in the bogs

...my buddies and me
on the deep blue sea

...or digging way down
dumb as a frown

...to find the root
with the heel of my boot

...and kick up dust
as a runaway must

...without such a circle
why bums we would be
filling the jerk hole
economy

with every ounce of our terrible crimes
signifying pennies and dimes...

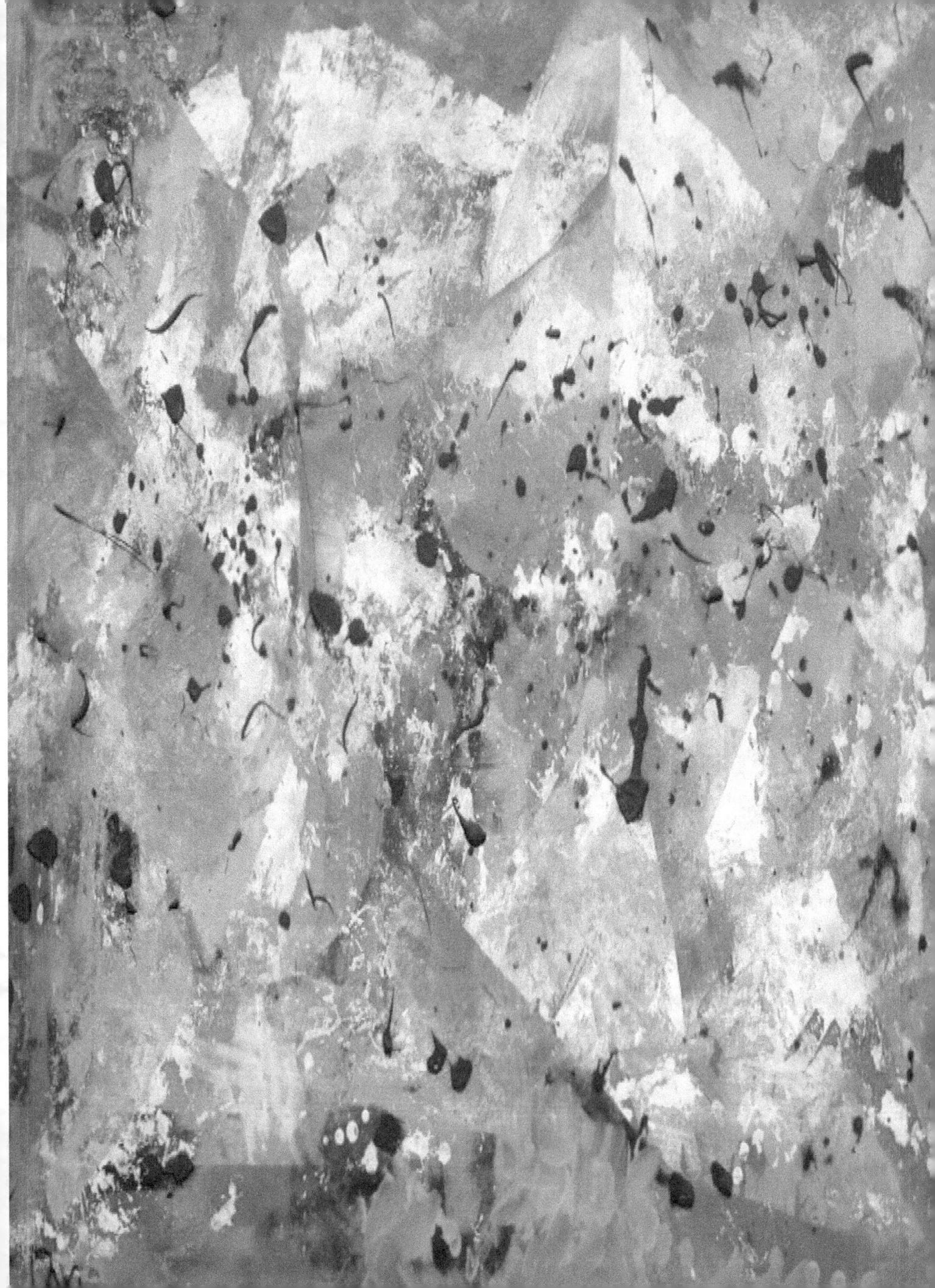

I WORK FOR YOU WITH MY NEUROTIC MIND

Cover art 'Starburst' by Rachel Davis (acrylic)

VISION FROM A KITCHEN PICTURE WINDOW

A verdance within the lavender bark of pine
...the child in me swells to tree and seed
till late summer begs for Autumn to come
...a vagrant bug...an egoless bum
charting the stumbling path outside with his eye
toward the richness within a morning sign
...stumbling and humming
a lullaby
while the cd performs that same classical tune
and the day unwinds
to an August moon.

WHAT ADOLESCENCE MEANS

A small garden of tree and weed
extends within cracked pavement
on a streets thin gutter

and the sun beats down
on such turbulence
among the ants and termites
or the passersby
whose cars moan with their engines
for an enigmatic sex.

This is Summer!
And love longs for drunkenness
...for ways to expand beyond
the stupid mind
a new semester keeps
in drilling deep the brain
for a chemistry of lesser knowledge
than human gods have died for
in the past.

We can recall these stories
in movies and in literature
with our own sweet fullness
to color and further fill the blanks

...but then soon the mind is dozy
for someone barely
more than a child in age

...and there is darkness...only darkness!
...to turn the other page.

MONKEY ON THE MOON

Monkey watches replays of the 1969 moonwalk
done in some bizarre video remake
with clusters of nudes

...he will be in the university in two years
studying advertising
because the soul of him
wants nothing unless
it is money.

Things are by nature uninteresting.

The other rich Dominican kids
find their passion
in vicarious
booze
and pornography
or slip off with a maid
or otherwise hungry and dark little girl
anxious for a marriage or settlement

...kids with everything think life is a game
and Monkey thinks
that they may
be right...but games
to him have lost
their meaning

except for those strange computer remakes
in virtual time
and kingdoms away
where fire has a different significance.

THOSE LESSER CRIMES OF NEW YORK

Little wonder that you steal a life
far away from Broadway songs
...their cheerful simple rights and wrongs
...a rat nose
poking around the garbage
discovers
of a mind deranged and loose

...so sad and wicked were these days
after a small weak will was shattered
so that nothing barely mattered
and the blood within the can
felt like rubbing alcohol

...yeah! All rubbish...weak and small
the meaning of the madness which was left.

At the bottom of the garbage pale
a glass shard like a rusty nail
far beyond fifth avenue
to indicate the smallness
of the theft.

I WORK FOR YOU WITH MY NEUROTIC MIND

I work for you with my neurotic mind
except to spend the gorgeous hours
in art with all its nature
in the concave of our love.

A plan made real by death
and yet too difficult to be designed
beyond the chaos of the trees and flowers
where fate unravels panting breath
whose sexual sighs reveal their powers

and make for you a painting
near the blanket where we dined.

I love this life
where chaos lifts us up
enough to gaze upon your beauty
in the million ways we work and cry
and drink and love and sup.

DRUGS FOR A TORTURED MIND

I wandered the streets...a whore for love
...my poems, a pastime for the ladies
and wrote my lonely heart at night.

The dogs, the cats, the rats with rabies
encircled me and drank my love
and ate my money with a knife

and buried bones and words I shared
and sent me to another life
...a pigeon in the morning light
of New York 's central square.

QUIET THINGS

When Summer begins to slip toward the Fall
A Tchaikovsky symphony muted to background
in the computer of my brain
while the typing keys
etch likewise words
in similar disease
to the flight of summer birds
making way for Autumn.

The music varies
...profoundly dark
or ebulent
...but as I say
...either way
toned down toward a passive restraint

in the dim day of a Saturday forgone.
Quiet things
tired
and yet desperate for some sure footed meaning
in a moment made for a song
near the season of our gleaning.

BEING MARRIED TO A WILDER NATURE

When you fly my nerves fly with you
...air born and infectious worries
climb my huge walls full of art
and kiss the icon
sacred and profane
where passions turn to care.

I fly prone and full of nettles!
lying here and bathed by computer violins
when you fly off
to see your children and their cities,
their cathedrals and their sins
their young and harried bodies
and their spirits full of air
much like the air which lifts your plane aloft.

When you ascend
above this globe where oceans stretch
and rivers bend
I fly through caverns underneath
the pictures that you etch
and leave with me to keep me
within my tearful token

and when you fly
you think only of the sky
and I think
of the engine
smashed and broken.

AN ART BEYOND ALL TRAGEDY

Twinkle and tear
in a goodnight kiss
sighing with rich and elderly beauty

...or the art on our walls
...your other bliss
...cubistic red
with eyes on fire!

There is this self portrait in our room
that dances when the computer screen flickers
...music too! A dancing choir!
....this silken loom that spins into knickers
a comedy of erotic laughter

till I fall asleep and dream of you
like a million voices
in the soul, in the brain,

in the sweetest pain
of our happy hereafter.

ACHE

From the day we leave the womb
and long before the heart stops and the bones decay
that physicality which propped
a wasteful mind and self made up that way
turns to natural forms and art
to a dry atonal music
and its whispered words in poems
to lug the load and pull the cart
of heavy meaning
and its rich cathedral stones
to that fortressed storm within
where things consider God
and all such power

as causes us to weep
and heap the tomb
with mercy prayers and flowers
from the day we leave the womb.

OLD MAN, FRONT SEAT, NEXT DOOR TO THE DRIVER

Breathe slowly
the air in plaza parking
...on the lilipad
the toad is barking
and sunlight sifts
this windsheild dream
whose light reflects
and goes to Mars

and a place quite vacant
men and cars.

MIAMI'S FIRE IN THE DARKNESS

A burning drug addicted urge
to push those words,
those images
toward white-out-
drunkenness,
among the alligators and the birds

...and sleep the afternoon till night
while such a brain keeps burning white!

LOVING THE GREATER PASSION

You curled up cat wise on the bed downstairs
...the theory was
that in a few hours I would tend to things
...though I did not because
the brooding smoke of evening
and a gnawing cough
followed my small anxieties
and wandered with my mind.

In the drowsy time
of four a.m.
while night ran into morning
full of cigarettes and wheezing
full of codeine dreams revealing
in the mind awake
computer screens which fill themselves
with poems the poet makes

...and art hung carefully on the wall!
...and denim housecoats for the Fall!
...in a house too difficult to maintain
yet kissed with purpose from the heart

while time decays
yet stays alive
and joyous
in its poignant dreams

and death and sleep are only distant thoughts
but soon to come for all of that.

I wait for you to paint a nude
...perhaps a portrait of yourself
sometime against this stale etude

and give me time to pause and sleep
in corners curled up
with the cat...!

SOLITUDE

Gorecki in the background
....orthodox and haunting
Christian depth into a vacant world
in symphonies of shadow.

Music in the dark of night
will sweeten thoughts in this glazed mind
and ease the pen, the will, the sex
into inscribing letters on the heart
which pull the moment up
with pulse and art

whose poet lies awake and stares
at corners of the vaunting
next to windows in a small room's world
above an Autumn meadow.